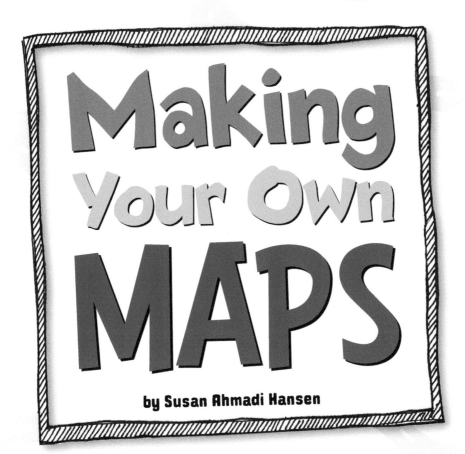

Making Your Own MAPS

by Susan Ahmadi Hansen

PEBBLE
a capstone imprint

Published by Pebble, an imprint of Capstone
1710 Roe Crest Drive, North Mankato, Minnesota 56003
capstonepub.com

Library of Congress Cataloging-in-Publication Data
Names: Hansen, Susan Ahmadi, author.
Title: Making your own maps / by Susan Ahmadi Hansen.
Description: North Mankato, Minnesota : Pebble, 2023. | Series: On the map | Includes bibliographical references and index. | Audience: Ages 5-8 | Audience: Grades K-1 | Summary: "Need help getting around your new neighborhood or school? A map can help! Learn how to make your own, and you'll be a pro at getting around a new place in no time! This interactive introduction to map-making will help kids build visual literacy skills and navigate their world"-- Provided by publisher.
Identifiers: LCCN 2022001135 (print) | LCCN 2022001136 (ebook) | ISBN 9781666349627 (hardcover) | ISBN 9781666349665 (paperback) | ISBN 9781666349702 (pdf) | ISBN 9781666349788 (kindle edition)
Subjects: LCSH: Cartography--Juvenile literature.
Classification: LCC GA105.6 .H36 2023 (print) | LCC GA105.6 (ebook) | DDC 526--dc23/eng20220711
LC record available at https://lccn.loc.gov/2022001135
LC ebook record available at https://lccn.loc.gov/2022001136

Editorial Credits
Editor: Ericka Smith; Designer: Tracy Davies; Media Researcher: Svetlana Zhurkin; Production Specialist: Katy LaVigne

Image Credits
Capstone: 5, Maps.com, 7, 8, 11, 19, Renée Doyle, 16; Capstone Studio: Karon Dubke, 15; Getty Images: Angelafoto, 17, Fly View Productions, 9, SW Productions, 4; Shutterstock: Anastasi Abel, cover background (left), BlueRingMedia, cover (hand), Elena Berd, 10, filborg, 13 (map), kosmofish (basketball), 11, 19, meimei studio, 16 (compass rose), pnDl, 13 (swing icon), Svetlana Kharchuk, cover background (right), Sylfida (groceries icon), 11, 19; Svetlana Zhurkin: 21

TABLE OF CONTENTS

Words in **bold** are in the glossary.

Why Make Your Own Map?

You've moved to a new neighborhood. And you want to know if there's a park nearby. Or maybe you're going to a new school. A map can help!

A map is like a picture of an area. It helps you learn about a place. It can also help you get around.

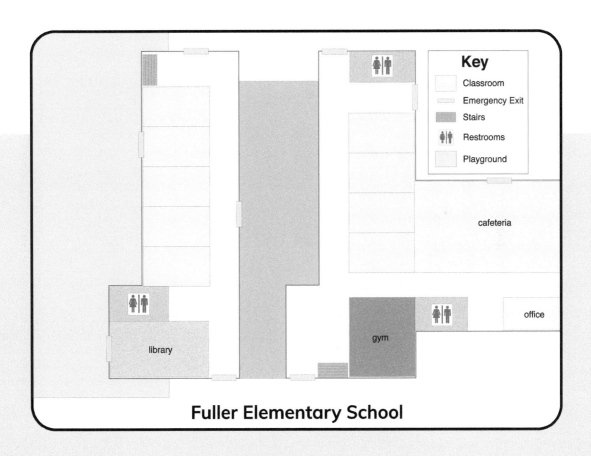

Fuller Elementary School

What's on a Map?

A map shows you where a place is. It also shows how far away a place is and how you can get there.

Landmarks, **symbols**, and **keys** help you find places. **Scales** and **compass roses** help you get there. You can make your own map using these tools!

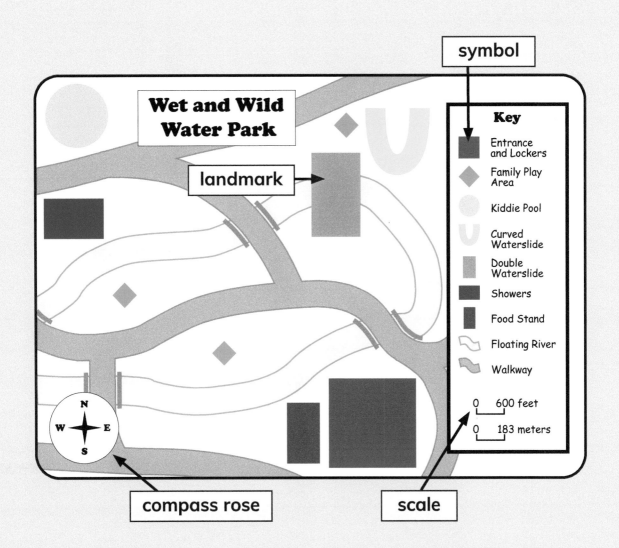

symbol

Wet and Wild Water Park

landmark

Key

Entrance and Lockers

Family Play Area

Kiddie Pool

Curved Waterslide

Double Waterslide

Showers

Food Stand

Floating River

Walkway

0   600 feet

0   183 meters

compass rose

scale

Scales

Say you want to draw a map of your neighborhood. How can it fit onto a piece of paper? Make it smaller! Draw a square on a sheet of paper. That's your home.

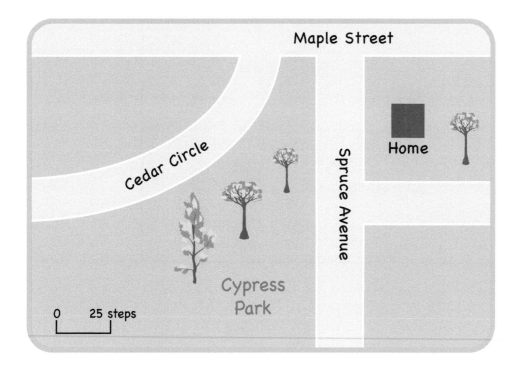

Scales tell how big things really are.

Walk 25 steps from home with a caregiver.

One inch on your map will show 25 steps.

Draw an inch-long line in a corner. Label it.

Landmarks

What else do you want to add to your map? A grocery store? Your school? The library? These are landmarks.

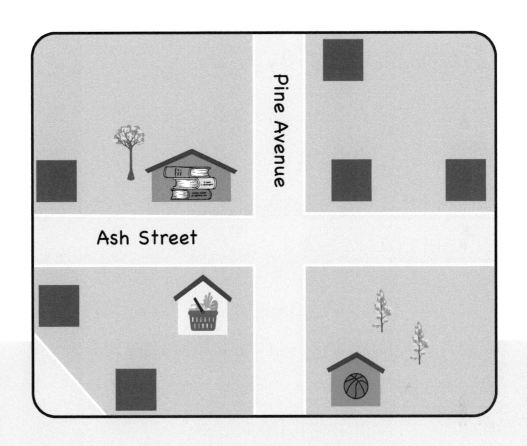

Landmarks are important places. You can see them easily. They help you figure out where you are.

Symbols and Keys

A symbol is a simple drawing that stands for something on a map. A square might stand for a house. A swing might show where a playground is.

Colors are used as symbols too. Blue can show rivers or lakes. Black lines can show streets. What symbols can you use for places in your neighborhood?

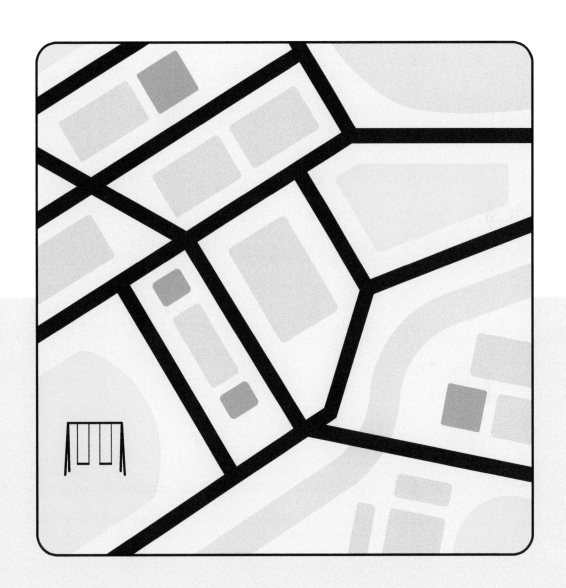

How will others know what the symbols mean? You need a key. A key shows the symbols and tells what they stand for.

Draw a box in a corner of your map. Inside the box, draw a picture for each symbol. Next to each symbol, write what it stands for.

15

Compass Roses

To use a map, you may need to know which way is north. The compass rose on a map shows directions. The arrows point north (N), south (S), east (E), and west (W).

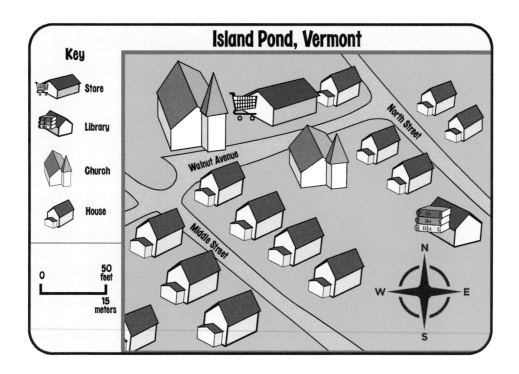

Use a compass to find north. What do you see outside your home when you are facing north? Draw a compass rose to show which way is north on your map.

Using Your Map

Your map is ready! Use it to get to school. First, find your home. Then, find your school.

Use your finger to trace a path. Look at the scale. How far away is your school? What landmarks are on your way? In which direction should you go first?

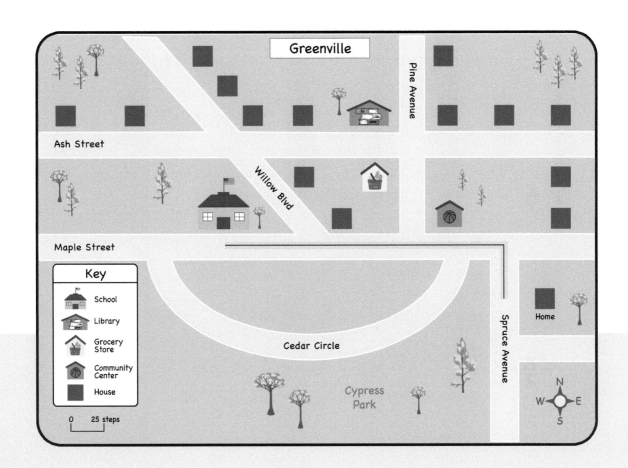

Make a Treasure Map

Try making a treasure map! Ask a caregiver to help you.

- small toys
- paper
- colored pencils, crayons, or markers
- compass

1. Pick a few spots at the park. Hide toys there.
2. Walk 25 steps in one direction from the last hiding spot. That can be 1 inch (2.54 centimeters) on your map.
3. Draw a scale (1 inch equals 25 steps) on your paper.
4. Use a compass to find north. Draw a compass rose.
5. Identify landmarks in the park.
6. Draw symbols to show where they are.

7. Draw a key to tell what the symbols mean.
8. Mark each hiding spot with an X.
9. Give the map to a friend. Can they find the treasures?

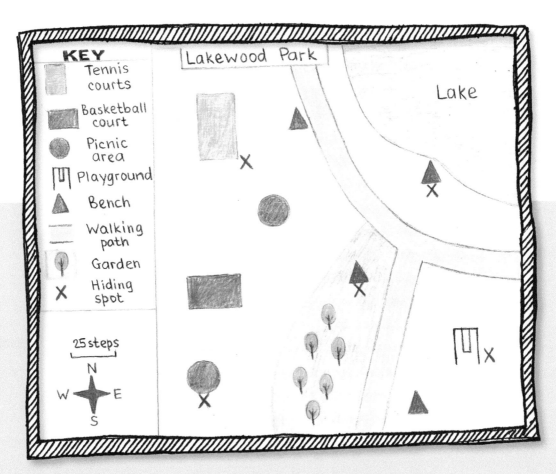

Glossary

compass rose (KUHM-puhs ROHZ)—a label that shows direction on a map

key (KEE)—a list that explains symbols

landmark (LAND-mark)—something that stands out, such as a big tree or a building

scale (SKALE)—a label on a map that compares the distances on a map with the actual distances on Earth

symbol (SIM-buhl)—a design or picture on a map that stands for something else

Read More

Brundle, Harriet. *Map My Community*. New York: Crabtree Publishing Company, 2018.

Dillemuth, Julie. *Mapping My Day*. Washington, D.C.: Magination Press, 2017.

Sweeney, Joan. *Me on the Map*. New York: Alfred A. Knopf, 2018.

Internet Sites

Google Earth
earth.google.com

Mr. Nussbaum: "Maptivation — Online Map Making"
mrnussbaum.com/maptivation-online-map-making

PBS: "Map Your Neighborhood"
pbs.org/parents/crafts-and-experiments/map-your-neighborhood

Index

About the Author

Susan Ahmadi Hansen is a children's writer and a teacher. She especially enjoys teaching young readers and writers to fall in love with books. Susan has four adult children who live on three different continents. She lives with her husband in Cedar Park, Texas.